ENCOURAGEMENT FROM
# 30,000
FEET

# ENCOURAGEMENT FROM
# 30,000
## FEET

Encouraging Stories from a Pilot's View

CAPTAIN GREG JOHNSTON

WESTBOW
PRESS®
A DIVISION OF THOMAS NELSON
& ZONDERVAN

WestBow Press books may be ordered through booksellers or by contacting:

WestBow Press
A Division of Thomas Nelson & Zondervan
1663 Liberty Drive
Bloomington, IN 47403
www.westbowpress.com
1 (866) 928-1240

Scripture taken from the New King James Version®. Copyright © 1982
by Thomas Nelson. Used by permission. All rights reserved.

This book is a work of non-fiction. Unless otherwise noted, the author and the publisher
make no explicit guarantees as to the accuracy of the information contained in this book
and in some cases, names of people and places have been altered to protect their privacy.

ISBN: 978-1-9736-1549-1 (sc)
ISBN: 978-1-9736-2299-4 (hc)
ISBN: 978-1-9736-1550-7 (e)

Library of Congress Control Number: 2018900646

Print information available on the last page.

WestBow Press rev. date: 3/7/2018

# FOREWORD

Greg brings a wheels-up perspective to readers willing to book a trip. His vantage point from the cockpit has been translated through the keyboard. A mile-high view on God, daily living, relationships, and faith struggles and victories makes this book worth the read. As a personal friend of Greg's, I know his heart is in each chapter, so I completely recommend this read.

—Reverend Eddie Kirby
(First United Methodist Church, Pascagoula, Mississippi)

# ACKNOWLEDGEMENT

First and foremost, I want to thank My Lord and Savior, Jesus Christ, without whom nothing would be possible.

I would also like to thank my wife, Beth, who encouraged me to write this book and has remained by my side on our flight of over thirty-seven years. Beth, you are the greatest encourager I know.

Finally, I want to dedicate this book to my daughter, Claire; my son, Lee; my daughter in law, Amber; and of course, my two awesome granddaughters, Locksley and Avery. You are truly God's gift to me and I love all of you more than words can describe.

# INTRODUCTION

Please allow me to introduce myself. My name is Greg Johnston. I am a captain with American Airlines. I was hired in 1986 by USAir, which merged with PSA, then Piedmont Airlines. Sometime later, after struggling financially, the company hired a new management team and changed the name to USAirways. Things were looking better until 9/11 happened. This, of course, changed everything for America, especially the airline industry. USAirways went through two bankruptcies and came very close to liquidating. Then came the next merger with America West Airlines, and although those were lean years, the company managed to obtain some stability. Finally, in December 2013, USAirways merged with American Airlines to form the largest airline in the world. That, in a nutshell, is a history of my airline career.

A lot of water has passed under the bridge in the past thirty-plus years, during which I've seen and experienced a lot of things. The greatest experience occurred in October 1988, when I reported for a trip with a captain whom I'd never met. I was a DC-9 first officer at the time and was living the dream. As we began the trip, the captain mentioned that he was a part-time full-gospel minister. My first thought was, "Oh great, three days with this guy." Interestingly enough, during that trip, it was I who would bring up theological questions, which he would answer by showing me passages in the Bible. It was shortly after that trip that I realized that Jesus Christ was who He claimed to be, and I received Him by faith in Him and what He accomplished through His death, burial, and resurrection.

Though I didn't totally grasp it (and never will), over the years I began to realize that, through the cross of Calvary, I became a new creation and that Jesus took all of my sin and gave me all of His righteousness (2 Corinthians 5:17–21).

I wish I could say that I was the greatest example of what a Christian was supposed to be, but that is not the case. What I can say, however, is that through all of my faults and failures, He has been faithful and patient, continually molding me into His image. I am and always will be a work in progress; and for that, I will always bow down and worship Him. I know now that it is only when I fall at His feet, and when I am dependent on Him and independent from this world, that I am truly in the highest place of all!

Over the years, I have seen a lot of people struggle with their faith journey and realized that, in many cases, a word of encouragement was all that was needed to change their situation. It is for this reason that I wanted to share with you some encouragement from thirty thousand feet. My prayer is that you will sense the anointing of the Holy Spirit in your life and that God will use these short stories to inspire and encourage you. Hopefully, these stories will help make your journey just a bit smoother.

# DAY 1—INDOCTRINATION

*See I am doing a new thing! Now it springs up; do you not receive it? I am making a way in the wilderness and streams in the wasteland.*

*—ISAIAH 43:19*

The date is May 5, 1986. I have completed the interview process and reported for indoctrination. I'm in Pittsburgh, Pennsylvania, and my wife and two-month-old son are in Montgomery, Alabama. I'm lonely and apprehensive as I begin a new and very different chapter in my life, and yet, this is the fulfillment of a dream that I have had since my first flight lesson in October 1973. It's quite interesting how this experience parallels another new and very different chapter—the one that began when I came to Christ. It also required indoctrination to learn what this new birth really means, along with the new values, new desires, and, yes, new struggles that were to follow. It was exciting and even somewhat scary; after all, everything I grew up believing was now subject to change. However, I was not without the teacher and comforter, the Holy Spirit. He led me to God's Word, to a church, and to a church family that would support and encourage me in my new journey.

What about you? Where are you in your journey? Have you gone through your indoctrination training? Have you read your ops manual, the Bible, the infallible Word of God? Are you surrounded by encouragers? If not, I would highly recommend finding positive, uplifting followers of Jesus Christ who will help you stay on course as you write your own new chapter.

Isaiah 43:19 says, "See I am doing a new thing! Now it springs up; do you not receive it? I am making a way in the wilderness and streams in the wasteland." This, of course, was God's word to the Jews, but could it be He's saying the same thing to you and me? Whether He's calling you to come to Him for the first time to make that new creation or calling you to grow and mature in the faith, the message is the same. God is doing a new thing in you. Don't miss it!

## PRAYER

Lord, thank You for showing us a new thing, giving me new values and desires. Thank You for Your Word, Your Spirit, and Your family, the body of Christ, to support and encourage me on my journey with You. Amen.

## NOTES

# NOTES

_____

_____

_____

_____

_____

_____

_____

_____

_____

_____

_____

_____

_____

_____

_____

_____

_____

_____

_____

_____

_____

_____

_____

_____

_____

_____

# DAY 2—THE MANUAL

*Do not conform any longer to the patterns of this world, but be
transformed by the renewing of your mind. Then you will be able to test
and approve what God's will is - His good, pleasing, and perfect will.*

—ROMANS 12:2

Well, indoctrination is over, and we have received our crew base and aircraft assignments. Being a Southern boy, for me, it made perfect sense to be based in … Boston, Massachusetts! If you knew how much I hate cold weather, you would be laughing right now. For me, anything below sixty degrees is unbearable! But Boston turned out to be a good experience, and I will always have good memories from my time there.

I was also assigned the DC-9 as a first officer, which was somewhat intimidating. After all, the largest aircraft I had flown up to that time was a Beechcraft King Air 300, a turboprop that carried 8 passengers, weighed 14,000 pounds, and cruised at 350 miles per hour. By contrast, the DC-9 carried 110 passengers, weighed 105,000 pounds, and cruised at 550 miles per hour. It was a whole new world of flying, and the only way to survive it was to study the flight manual and follow standard operating procedures.

Here's the reality: I became a pilot the first time I soloed that Piper Cherokee 140 back in 1973. What changed was my growth and understanding, which would come only as I learned how to operate the aircraft by studying the manual, learning the flight profiles, and knowing the normal and emergency procedures—and finally, by putting to use everything I had learned as I flew the line.

The same is true in our walk with the Lord. How can we be Christlike if we never read about Him and learn His nature? On the other hand, what good would we be if all we did was study constantly and never flew the line in real life?

We all have seasons where we don't study the manual like we should, and maybe we don't even fly the way we should. Those things happen because life sometimes gets in the way. It's up to us to schedule—daily, preferably—time to prayerfully spend time with the Lord and in His Word. And then we must walk boldly—though not arrogantly—in His ways so others can see Christ in us!

As the scripture from Romans 12:2 states, it is important that we realize that God is calling us to constantly be renewing our minds through reading His Word, receiving good preaching, and the teaching of godly teachers who are mature in their faith. It is through that constant renewing that we cease being conformed to this temporary world and begin to know what God's good, pleasing, and perfect will is.

If greater knowledge of the aircraft and the manual made me a better DC-9 pilot, how much more will having a greater knowledge of the Lord and His Word make us better Christians?

## PRAYER

Heavenly Father, I thank You again for Your Word, which is constantly changing and renewing my mind to conform to Your will. As I receive Your Word and walk boldly in Your ways, I pray that others will see the reflection of Christ and His love, thereby being drawn to Him. Amen.

## NOTES

---

# DAY 3—FUEL FOR POWER

My people are destroyed for lack of knowledge ...

—HOSEA 4:6

And my God shall supply all your need according
to His riches in glory by Christ Jesus.

—PHILIPPIANS 4:19

The aircraft I currently fly are the Airbus 319, 320, and 321. The 321 weighs approximately 205,000 pounds at its maximum takeoff weight, with each engine delivering approximately 33,000 pounds of thrust; the maximum fuel capacity is 52,500 pounds, or just under 8,000 gallons. In the present configuration, the plane carries 187 passengers with a crew of 6 for a total of 193 people. Needless to say, that's a lot of weight to lift off the ground, climb to a maximum altitude of 39,000 feet, and fly coast to coast at over 500 miles per hour. It also goes without saying that between the fuel and the engine, there is a potential for a tremendous amount of energy to be activated.

Now just imagine a man from the nineteenth century taking a seat in the cockpit. He would have no idea what he has at his fingertips. And in fact, if he were going on a long trip, he would want to get out of the plane and get on his horse to begin the journey. He would spend weeks to months to travel distances that could be traveled in just a few short hours in the Airbus. Just imagine—because of his lack of understanding, all of that potential power and speed was not used. Isn't it the same for the believer? Hosea reminds us that God's people are destroyed for lack of knowledge. The apostle Paul tells us that our God, through Christ, shall supply all our needs. He has "fueled" us with His Word and given us the power of the Holy Spirit, who lives in us. The Holy Spirit will enable us to climb above any circumstance in which we may find ourselves! Are you struggling with something in your life and feel like the more you struggle, the worse it gets? When you get on an aircraft, how much do you struggle to fly? The fact is that you don't struggle at all. You merely sit down, relax, and put your faith in the manufacturer, the mechanics, the pilots, and the air traffic controllers to get you to your destination safely and on time. In reality, if you didn't have faith in the people and the system, you wouldn't even get on the aircraft.

Well, the same is true in life and in our walk with God. The more we understand that He has already supplied all of our needs through His riches by Christ, the more victory we will have in this life! Let's be encouraged today because our God has already given us the fuel and the power. It is now up to us to have our tanks filled by faith.

### PRAYER

Thank You, Lord, for supplying me with power for this incredible journey. Help me gain a greater understanding of the depth of Your power as I receive it by faith. Amen.

### NOTES

_____

_____

_____

_____

_____

_____

_____

# NOTES

_____

_____

_____

_____

_____

_____

_____

_____

_____

_____

_____

_____

_____

_____

_____

_____

_____

_____

_____

_____

_____

_____

_____

_____

# DAY 4—PREFLIGHT

Finally my brethren, be strong in the Lord and in the power
of His might. Put on the whole armor of God, that you
may be able to stand against the wiles of the devil.

—EPHESIANS 6:10-11

Before every flight, we check the aircraft to make sure it's fit to fly the next leg. One pilot performs a walk-around to check the conditions of the tires, engines, wings, tail, and fuselage for any damage or excessive wear. The other pilot checks the fuel, oil, and hydraulic levels from gauges in the cockpit, and this pilot then initializes the navigation computers. Both pilots then check various other systems, and then together, they perform the before-start checklist to be sure everything is checked prior to pushing off the gate.

In addition to checking the aircraft, each pilot must do a self-assessment to be sure he or she is also fit to fly. The biggest concerns for pilots are fatigue and health. It is our responsibility to get off the trip if there is anything that hinders the performance of our duties. The same is true for us as believers. We are reminded in Ephesians 6:11 to "put on the full armor of God so that you can take your stand against the devil's schemes." The armor consists of the belt of truth, the breastplate of righteousness, and the shoes of the gospel of peace. To complete the armor, we have the shield of faith, the helmet of salvation, and the sword of the Spirit, which is the word of God!

Whether we are going to fly on a clear day with blue skies or on a day when we'll have to do battle with weather, we will always perform our preflight inspections. Should we do any less when it comes to our daily walk in this world? You may be on top of the world today or you may be going through the darkest time of your life. Either way, you will need the protection of God's mighty armor at all times!

## PRAYER

Father, as I go out today, I know that I am ready for anything that comes my way because I have put on Your armor that protects and empowers me to live victoriously. For that, I give You thanks, in Jesus's name. Amen.

## NOTES

_____

_____

_____

_____

_____

_____

_____

_____

_____

_____

_____

_____

_____

_____

_____

_____

## NOTES

# DAY 5—TRUST

All Scripture is given by inspiration of God, and is profitable for doctrine,
for reproof, for correction, for instruction in righteousness, that the man
of God may be complete, thoroughly equipped for every good work.

— 2 TIMOTHY 3:16-17

As I write this, I am sitting in the back of an aircraft, commuting home after flying for the last five days. Riding in the cabin is not my favorite place. I'd rather be in the cockpit, flying. It's a control issue, I know. The reality is that it takes faith to fly as a passenger; yet it's not blind faith. It's faith in a system that has served the aviation industry well for many years. The fact is that the captain didn't just show up yesterday with a license purchased online. He or she must have the minimum number of hours required to qualify for the Airline Transport Pilot rating and pass a written test along with a check ride that must be passed in order to obtain the rating. (The ATP rating is the equivalent to a PhD since it is the highest rating one can earn as a pilot.) In addition to that, the captain must pass recurring check rides every year. The system works quite well, and because of that, we climb aboard and put our lives in the flight crew's hands. Again, it is faith but not blind faith!

Some people say that it takes blind faith to believe that the Bible is God's Word. In fact, nothing could be further from the truth. The Bible is actually a library of sixty-six books and letters that were determined to be inspired because of many reasons. For example, there is the issue of historical accuracy, which they contain. Then there are hundreds of early manuscripts—more, in fact, than other literary works that are also held in high esteem. There are hundreds of prophecies that were fulfilled hundreds of years after they were written. Also, those sixty-six books are intertwined to tell one story, and that is the redemption of man through the death, burial, and resurrection of Jesus Christ! There are virtually unlimited sources of evidence that point to the reliability and truth of the scriptures. The point I want to make here is that ours is not a blind faith; it is one that is both reasonable and sure. It is also a faith that we can rest comfortably in because it has and will continue to withstand the test of time. Hebrews 4:12 reminds us that God's Word is "living and powerful, and sharper than any two-edged sword" and that it discerns "the thoughts and intents of the heart." Second Timothy 3:16 also assures us that "all scripture is given by inspiration of God."

So here's the bottom line for me: If I can trust my life to the captain of the plane I'm riding on based on what I know about the system, how much more can I trust my eternal destiny on the truth of the death, burial, and resurrection of Christ based on the evidence that's available for all to see? Is this a blind faith? Hardly!

## PRAYER

Lord, thank You for Your Word that is alive and equips us for our life's journey. Father, I trust not only my life but my eternal destiny to the fact that Your Word is eternal, infallible, and inerrant. Thank You for revealing to me such a strong foundation that I can truly walk in confidence knowing that You are in control. Amen.

## NOTES

_____

_____

_____

_____

# NOTES

_____

_____

_____

_____

_____

_____

_____

_____

_____

_____

_____

_____

_____

_____

_____

_____

_____

_____

_____

_____

_____

_____

_____

_____

_____

# DAY 6—THE CAPTAIN'S VOICE

Now when He got into a boat, His disciples followed Him. And
suddenly a great tempest arose on the sea, so that the boat was covered
with the waves. But He was asleep. Then His disciples came to Him
and awoke Him, saying, "Lord, save us! We are perishing!"
But He said to them, "Why are you fearful, O you of little faith?" Then He arose
and rebuked the winds and the sea, and there was a great calm. So the men
marveled, saying, "Who can this be, that even the winds and sea obey Him?"

—MATTHEW 8:23-27

It was a dark and stormy night several years ago as we were preparing
to fly from Charlotte, NC to Washington, DC. In fact, we were
delayed for several minutes as a line of severe thunderstorms passed
through Charlotte. Once cleared for takeoff but before we took the
runway, I made an announcement to our passengers letting them
know that we would experience some turbulence. I also mentioned
that they would be seeing a lot of lightning reflecting through the
clouds as we made our way up to Washington but that we would
remain clear of all the severe weather with our onboard weather
radar.

As we continued north, we encountered mostly light turbulence
along with a lot of lightning reflecting through the clouds. I made
more announcements to let the passengers know that even though
they were seeing a lot of lightning, we were, in fact, several miles
away from any severe weather and that it would clear up around
Richmond. Once we got to Richmond, we broke out into the clear,
and the remainder of the flight was smooth and in clear skies.

I thought nothing more of what we just experienced. However, as the passengers were deplaning, a lady stopped to thank me for talking to them as we were flying through the weather. She was practically in tears as she explained how just hearing my voice reassured her we had everything under control and that we would weather the storm safely.

Life, just like that night, brings storms into our lives. As believers, we are not immune from those storms, but we also have a captain who reassures us that we will weather the storms of life because He is in absolute control. Matthew 8:23-27 tells us about the time the disciples encountered a storm while in their boat. In the midst of the storm, Jesus got up and rebuked the wind and the waves, and immediately it was calm.

Are you going through a dark night and gripped by fear, not knowing what's ahead? Be encouraged; we are not without a captain. He will not only navigate us safely around those storms, He can actually calm them! If you listen closely, you can hear His reassuring voice saying, "Peace; be still!"

The storms hear His voice. Do we? Let's listen …

## PRAYER

Heavenly Father, as I go through the storms of life, help me hear Your voice as You speak to the storms and to my spirit, saying, "Peace, be still." I know, Lord, that You're the only one who can give me the peace that passes all understanding, and I thank You for it, in Jesus's name. Amen.

## NOTES

_____

_____

# NOTES

# DAY 7—OPPOSING FORCES

Therefore we also, since we are surrounded by so great a cloud of witnesses, let us lay aside every weight, and the sin which so easily ensnares us, and let us run with endurance the race that is set before us, looking unto Jesus, the author and finisher of our faith, who for the joy that was set before Him endured the cross, despising the shame, and has sat down at the right hand of the throne of God.

—HEBREWS 12:1-2

One of the first things we learn as pilots is that there are four forces that act on an aircraft in flight. Those four forces are lift, weight, thrust, and drag. Lift and weight are opposing forces, as are thrust and drag. In simple terms, if an aircraft has more lift created by its wings than its weight, a climb will result. On the other hand, if the lift is less than the weight, a descent will occur. Also, if thrust created by the engine exceeds the drag created by the airframe, an increase in speed results. If drag exceeds thrust, then a decrease in speed results.

From an operational standpoint, pilots must always ensure that the weight of the passengers, fuel, and baggage do not exceed performance limitations that are dictated by the length of the runway, airport elevation, and weather conditions at the time of takeoff.

During winter operations, another concern is icing. Icing decreases lift and increases drag by changing the shape and surface of the wings. It also increases the weight of the aircraft, and, in extreme cases, it can cause engine problems, which will decrease thrust. It is the responsibility of the captain to make sure that none of these issues hinder our flight.

In a sense, we have those same forces working on us that determine our flight path in everyday living. Hebrews 12:1–2 talks about enduring a race that is set before us. Perhaps if the writer of Hebrews had been a pilot, he would be referring to a flight we are about to take. In order to endure the race or flight, we are told to lay aside every weight and sin that so easily ensnares us. There are two of the forces (weight and drag) that are hindering our flights in life, things that are dragging us down and preventing us from taking flight. Each of us are weighed down by concerns, which could include finances, relationships, jobs, etc. We all experience sins that easily tempt and entangle us—some big, some small—but all are always at the door, looking for a way to enter our lives.

I have good news! We serve a great God and a mighty Savior who gives grace to His children! The writer here simply tells us to do two things. First, he says to throw off everything that weighs us down; in other words, get rid of the baggage. Just remove it from your life, throw it in the lost baggage container, and let it go! Secondly, he tells us to "fix our eyes on Jesus, the author and finisher of our faith." He's the only one who can provide the power (the thrust and lift) that will allow us to take flight! Some would say that laying aside every weight and sin is hard to do. I agree! In fact, I would say it is impossible! That's the very reason we are told to fix our eyes on Jesus. Living the Christian life is not difficult; it's impossible. The reality is that there is only one person who has ever done it, and that was Christ Himself. The only way that we can take this flight is by allowing Him to live in and through us! Be encouraged. Beginning today, we can take our eyes off of our baggage, our sin, and whatever our circumstances are, and firmly fix them on Jesus. In my spirit, I can hear Him making His boarding announcement for our flight. I'm getting on board. Will you join me?

## PRAYER

Lord Jesus, I am reminded that I can't live the Christian life unless I throw away everything that gets in the way and fix my eyes on You! Help me turn from the world and turn to You every day of my life. Thank You for Your love and grace that enables me to fly far above my circumstances. For that, I give You praise and glory. Amen.

## NOTES

_____

_____

_____

_____

_____

_____

_____

_____

_____

_____

_____

_____

_____

_____

_____

_____

_____

_____

_____

_____

_____

# NOTES

# DAY 8—THE NIGHT SKY

The heavens declare the glory of God; And the firmament shows His handiwork.

—PSALM 19:1

Flying from Albuquerque to Charlotte one night, I was amazed by the number of planets and stars that were visible. A few thousand years ago, the psalmist was also moved and wrote in Psalm 8:1, "O, Lord, our Lord, how excellent is Your name in all the earth, Who have set your glory above the heavens!" Later in Psalm 19:1, he wrote, "The heavens declare the glory of God."

The psalmist penned those verses while sitting on the side of a hill and looking at the night sky without the aid of a telescope. Today, we have radio-telescopes and the Hubble telescope, which shows stars and galaxies the psalmist could not have even imagined. Sadly, many people today look at those images with the view that they came out of some cosmic bang that had nothing to do with a Creator. I used to believe the same thing before I came to Christ. Now, I look into the skies and at the deep space images and stand in absolute awe at the majesty and power of Almighty God! In fact, it would not surprise me at all if, in all the planets, in all the galaxies, in all the universe, that we are the only life forms in existence!

Now stay with me here. Just imagine: the Creator of everything, in order to declare His glory, has created the entire infinite universe to display that glory! It's just amazing to me! Now I can't be dogmatic about that. After all, I haven't been to all of the planets yet to verify it. Think about it, though. Of all the billions of planets in all the universe, which one is He coming back to? Earth! Of all the planets in all the universe, on which one is He going to establish His kingdom? Earth! It's absolutely mind-boggling when you really dwell on it! If this is true, then what does it say about our awesome and magnificent God? Just imagine the extreme lengths He has gone through just to show us who He is! Yet, as inconceivable as it is to even attempt to grasp His majesty and Glory through the creation, all of that pales in comparison to His revealing of Himself through His only begotten Son, Jesus Christ, who revealed not only His power, but also His love, mercy, and grace.

The next time you look up into the night sky, think about how the infinite heavens declare the infinite glory of our infinite God, who has set His glory far above the heavens; and yet He cares about us so much that He knows the number of hairs on our heads. Be encouraged. After all, He created the universe. Surely He is able to handle anything that comes our way.

## PRAYER

Lord, when I consider the vastness of space, something that is far beyond my comprehension, I am truly overwhelmed at Your glory. And yet, You are mindful of me and even know the very number of hairs on my head. I can do nothing but fall on my face and worship You in all Your glory! Thank you, Father, for making me Your child, not because I deserved it, because I certainly didn't, but because You love me with a perfect love, through Christ my Lord. Amen.

## NOTES

# NOTES

# DAY 9—THE UNIFORM

For you are all sons of God through faith in Jesus Christ. For as
many of you who were baptized into Christ have put on Christ.

—GALATIANS 3:26-27

As I write today, I am in my hotel room in Syracuse, New York. In a few hours, I will have put on my uniform, gone down to the lobby, met my crew, and caught the hotel van to the airport to fly the last leg of my trip back to Charlotte, where I am based.

One of the things I have to be aware of as the captain and in uniform is that people who have never met me, and certainly don't know me, see the uniform and immediately form an opinion about me. Personally, I want to make the best impression I can because that uniform represents my profession, which I worked very hard to get into, and the company, which pays me for my service. In addition to that, I know that, statistically speaking, there's at least one person who has never flown before and others who are afraid to fly. To these passengers, my appearance and actions will go a long way in putting them at ease for their flight. To them, my identity is an airline captain.

I have to say that being an airline pilot has been a very fulfilling career. I'm very thankful to have had the opportunity to achieve my boyhood dream of flying for a major airline. However, my identity is not that of being a pilot. That is only my profession. In fact, my identity is being a child of God, which is far, far greater. Being a pilot is awesome! The benefits are great, but they can't begin to compare with the benefits of being a child of God!

Consider this: according to Paul's letter to the Ephesians, as a child of God, I have been blessed with every spiritual blessing in Christ. I was chosen in Christ before the foundation of the world. I am accepted, I have redemption through His blood, and my sins are forgiven. I have obtained an inheritance, and I have been sealed with the Holy Spirit, who is the guarantor of my inheritance. I have been raised up and now seated in the heavenly places with Christ. I have been saved by grace as a gift of God. I have been brought near to God by the blood of Christ, and I'm a fellow citizen of the household of God!

Wearing the uniform is something I enjoy doing, but one day, I will wear it for the last time and then I will no longer be a captain. However, back in 1988, I *put on Christ*; and that's one uniform I will never have to put away for it is eternal! Yes, in a couple of hours, my passengers will see me in my uniform, and they will identify me as the captain of their aircraft. But my prayer is that through my actions, they will know that I have put on Christ because it is in Him, and in Him alone, that I have my true eternal identity.

What about you? What's your identity? We can all get caught up in what we do, but the day is coming for all of us when we will no longer be able to put on our *uniform*. Wouldn't today be a good time to make sure we have put on Christ by faith in Him and His accomplished work on the cross? After all, it's the only uniform that is everlasting!

Be encouraged today, knowing that "neither death nor life, nor angels nor principalities, nor powers, nor things present nor things to come, nor height nor depth, nor any other created thing, shall be able to separate us from the love of God which is in Christ Jesus our Lord" (Romans 8:38–39).

## PRAYER

Heavenly Father, thank You for revealing the truth of my new identity in Christ. I also thank You for showing me that the only way I can truly represent You is by allowing Him to live through me. Lord, my desire is that when others see me, they will see Christ in me—the only hope of glory. Change me, mold me, and use me for Your glory. In Jesus's name. Amen.

## NOTES

_____

_____

_____

_____

_____

_____

_____

_____

_____

_____

_____

_____

_____

_____

_____

_____

_____

_____

# NOTES

_____

_____

_____

_____

_____

_____

_____

_____

_____

_____

_____

_____

_____

_____

_____

_____

_____

_____

_____

_____

_____

_____

_____

_____

# DAY 10—CRM

And if one member suffers, all the members suffer with it; or if
one member is honored, all the members rejoice with it. Now
you are the body of Christ, and members individually.

—1 CORINTHIANS 12:26-27

When I began my airline career over thirty years ago, the flight deck was a much different place than it is today. The pilot flying the aircraft was expected to know practically everything there was to know about the aircraft, including technical things that were totally unnecessary and contributed nothing to the safe conduct of flying the aircraft. The emergency procedures had several memory items that had to be accomplished rapidly and in the proper order, solely by memory. Of course, this was also a time when the workload and stress were at their highest. Decisions were made very quickly, with little or no interaction between the captain and the first officer, all at a time when interaction was most needed. Sadly, several accidents over the course of the years could have been avoided if more input between the two pilots had been used.

Fortunately, pilots have developed a system that has radically changed how the flight of an airliner is managed. We developed a way of getting both pilots involved and coordinated so they could work as a team, sharing the workload. This would prevent or capture mistakes before they cause an incident or accident. The system is referred to as Crew Resource Management or CRM. For example, years ago a pilot was expected to fly the aircraft and handle the emergency checklist with virtually no assistance from the other pilot. Today, if an emergency occurs, one pilot flies the aircraft, and the other handles the emergency checklist and manages the emergency. That way, someone is solely committed to keeping the aircraft in the air, which, of course, is the number one priority. CRM will also include interaction with the flight attendants, company flight dispatchers, maintenance, and finally, the air traffic controllers. All these resources are expected to be used in order to bring the aircraft back to the ground safely.

As believers, we also have a system of CRM, which could be called a Christian Resource Management system. Paul refers to the church as the body of Christ. In 1 Corinthians 12, he tells us that, even though we are one body, we are made up of many parts. Just as the human body is made up different parts, such as hands, eyes, ears, etc., so is the body of Christ. No human body could have just hands or legs or eyes and function. It must, instead, have all its parts to properly perform any tasks. God does not intend for us to perform alone. Instead, He has put the body of Christ together, giving all of us gifts from the Holy Spirit to be used to build up the body. In other words, He has ordained a type of CRM that brings all our spiritual resources together so that we can live in victory.

The body of Christ has teachers to teach us, preachers to proclaim God's word, along with other gifts to minister to His people. We need each other to encourage, support, and, yes, even to correct us. When we allow God's CRM to be used, lives are changed, relationships are built, and the lost are found. How is your CRM? I know mine could certainly improve! There is a song called "The Servant Song" that has a verse that says, "Brother, let me be your servant." This refers to us helping or serving other believers, but later, it adds, "May I have the grace to let you be my servant too." If you're like me, it's much easier to help someone than it is to ask for or receive help from them. Perhaps today you're in a place where you can help someone or maybe you could use some help. Either way, let's avoid being loners in our walk and allow God to teach us how to use His CRM so that when the next emergency in life occurs, the result will also be a safe landing.

## PRAYER

Lord, I'm reminded that although life is filled with trials and tribulations, we are never expected to go through them alone. Not only are You with us, You have surrounded us with the body of Christ, made up of others who love You and one another. Help me be more available to others when they are hurting, and give me grace to receive help from others when I am hurting. Amen.

## NOTES

# NOTES

_____

_____

_____

_____

_____

_____

_____

_____

_____

_____

_____

_____

_____

_____

_____

_____

_____

_____

_____

_____

_____

_____

_____

_____

_____

_____

# DAY 11—SITUATIONAL AWARENESS

*Finally brethren, whatever things are true, whatever things are noble, whatever things are just, whatever things are pure, whatever things are lovely, whatever things are of good report, if there is any virtue and if there is anything praiseworthy—meditate on these things.*

—PHILIPPIANS 4:8

As pilots, we must always be aware of what's going on with our aircraft. However, just being aware of our aircraft is not enough. We must also be aware of our surroundings. For example, after the ground crew completes our pushback from our departure gate, and before we begin our taxi to the runway, the first officer will check his or her side of the aircraft and announce, "Clear right," indicating there is nothing obstructing that side of the aircraft and that it is safe to taxi. I will also check my side and announce, "Clear left," indicating the same for my side. I will then begin our taxi to the assigned runway. We will use the same procedure before crossing runways and taking the runway for takeoff, even though the controller gives us permission to do so. We continue to maintain this type of vigilance throughout all phases of flight by listening to all conversations on the radio and, of course, watching outside for other planes and any threatening weather conditions. We refer to this as *situational awareness*.

The same need for being aware of our surroundings applies to life. Whether we are walking in a parking lot, paying attention to our surroundings for possible muggers, being in a crowd watching for any possible terrorist activity, or even being aware of what's occurring on a global scale, situational awareness is something we should all practice.

Today, I want us to focus on something that affects us on a more personal level: relationships with others. We all have relationships that are both positive and negative. We all have friends and family members who either build us up or tear us down. As believers, we are called to be salt and light in a dark and decaying world. Paul reminds us we should not have fellowship (close relationship) with unbelievers. Instead, we are to have fellowship with other believers in order to be built up and encouraged, no matter what we are dealing with at the time (2 Corinthians 6:14).

What kind of situation do you find yourself in today? If you're being torn down and constantly ridiculed, ask the Lord to give you a Holy Spirit situational awareness that will expose relationships that are depressing or even destructive, and then ask Him to lead you to those who are positive and encouraging. Pray for discernment concerning those negative relationships to help determine if you can be used by Him to bring about a positive change or if you need to cut the ties and move on.

Maybe you're in a low place now and aren't aware that those who are negatively influencing you are part of the problem. Paul reminds us in Romans 15:2 that we are to build our neighbors up. In Philippians 4:8, he further says that that we should focus on things that are positive and uplifting. Be encouraged; our Lord is here to help raise your situational awareness and has provided the body of Christ, His church, to build you up and help strengthen you for every challenge you will face.

## PRAYER

Lord, I must confess that with all the negativity and fear that is surrounding us in the world today, things can look pretty bleak. I know, however, that You haven't given me a spirit of fear and that I don't need to be controlled by my surroundings or those who want to bring me down. I thank You for Your Word, which gives me discernment concerning my relationships with others, and the assurance that You are in control. I can rest assured that since You are for me, I am more than a conqueror through Christ Jesus, my Lord and Savior. Amen.

## NOTES

# NOTES

_____

_____

_____

_____

_____

_____

_____

_____

_____

_____

_____

_____

_____

_____

_____

_____

_____

_____

_____

_____

_____

_____

_____

_____

_____

_____

# DAY 12—PERCEPTION

*Trust in the Lord with all your heart, And lean not on your own understanding;*
*In all your ways acknowledge Him, And He shall direct your paths.*

—PROVERBS 3:5-6

One of the greatest dangers for new pilots is a phenomenon known a spatial disorientation. Spatial disorientation, or vertigo, occurs when untrained pilots venture into weather such as fog or clouds that causes them to lose visual reference to the horizon. Without visual reference to the horizon, it is impossible to determine if you're turning, climbing, or descending. It's very difficult for anyone who hasn't experienced vertigo to even imagine how it could occur. A major part of the problem is due to the fact that an aircraft moves up and down in addition to left and right; and the gravitational forces that one experiences in an aircraft can introduce all kinds of deceptive feelings on the human body that can cause wrong perceptions that, if left unchecked, will almost surely result in an accident in just a few short minutes. That is why there is a restriction placed on new pilots that restrains them from flying into areas of reduced visibility.

It's only after many hours of intense training that pilots learn to use and trust their flight instruments that they are certified to fly in clouds, fog, and other forms of inclement weather. In fact, with experience, it actually becomes second nature and perfectly safe to do so.

Did you know that the same principle applies to our walk with God? Perception plays a major role in how we relate to God and, in turn, to others. You see, despite the fact that we have received Christ as our Savior, we have a deceiver who will promote lies. These give false perceptions that say that we aren't good enough and that our heavenly Father won't use or bless us. If we allow those feelings to persist and control us, we too will face a spiritual vertigo, causing us to lose our direction and suffer defeat.

The truth is that God has given us His instrument to direct us, regardless of how we feel. That instrument is His Word, the Bible. God's Word will always guide us, no matter what our feelings, if only we trust and apply it by faith. In many ways, a believer's trust in the Bible and a pilot's trust in his flight instruments are the same; it is increased through experience and practice. Just as a pilot must spend hours in the cockpit, learning to trust the flight instruments, we need to spend time in God's Word, allowing the Holy Spirit to lead us into the truth rather than trusting our feelings, allowing them to deceive us and lead us into unbelief.

Perhaps you've had a time in your life when you felt like you've failed God and have fallen out of relationship with Him, and that there's no way you could ever be acceptable to Him again. May I just say, that's a lie straight from the enemy and an absolute false perception. Think about it: as believers, our right standing with God is dependent on what Christ did for us at Calvary, not on what we do. I encourage you today to not allow your perception of your righteousness determine your relationship with God. Instead, allow God's Word, His truth, to determine your perception of your righteousness because it's only when your perception lines up with God's Word that you will enjoy the peace that exceeds all understanding and walk in victory! Philippians 4:7 reminds us that the peace of God will guard our hearts and minds in Christ Jesus. Which will you believe: your feelings or His truth? Your answer to that will determine your course and, ultimately, your destiny!

## PRAYER

Heavenly Father, as I journey through life, I realize that there are many distractions that can divert me from Your will and direction. Thank You for giving me Your Word, which keeps me on course. Help me hear Your voice and sense Your very presence every day as I walk by faith. Amen.

## NOTES

_____

_____

_____

_____

_____

_____

_____

_____

_____

_____

_____

_____

_____

_____

_____

_____

_____

_____

# NOTES

_____

_____

_____

_____

_____

_____

_____

_____

_____

_____

_____

_____

_____

_____

_____

_____

_____

_____

_____

_____

_____

_____

_____

_____

_____

_____

# DAY 13—FASTEN YOUR SEATBELT

Therefore whoever hears these sayings of Mine, and does them, I
will liken him to a wise man who built his house on the rock: and
the rain descended, the floods came, and the winds blew and beat on
that house; and it did not fall, for it was founded on the rock.

—MATTHEW 7:24-25

If you've ever flown, I'm sure you've heard the captain make an announcement similar to this: "Ladies and gentlemen, we have reached our cruising altitude, and since we're having a smooth ride, I'm going to turn the seatbelt sign off, so you're free to move about the cabin as necessary. I do want to remind you, however, that it is a requirement to keep your seatbelts fastened anytime you're seated, just in case we encounter any unexpected turbulence." As pilots, we can usually predict if our flight will be smooth or turbulent. We use many sources to evaluate what kind of turbulence we will encounter. To begin with, our flight release will show the turbulence forecast along our route. We can also get a good idea just by looking at the different cloud formations, and finally, we will check with the air traffic controllers who are talking to other aircraft and receiving ride reports from those aircraft. With all those resources, we can get a good picture of what to expect. However, we are sometimes surprised by the unexpected turbulence that can be somewhat uncomfortable and, in some cases, can cause injuries to those who aren't seated with fastened seatbelts. That's why we always stress the importance of keeping your seatbelts fastened at all times in-flight.

Life also has a nasty habit of giving us some unexpected turbulence. Sometimes it's just some small bumps; on other occasions, it's severe turbulence that can cause serious injuries if we aren't belted down with the Word of God. Jesus spoke of the house that was built on the sandy foundation of unbelief and the one that was built on the rock of faith in God's Word (Matthew 7). Both houses experienced the storm. The one built on sand was destroyed, but the one built on the rock of faith withstood the storm's might. We would all like to have a smooth flight in this life. Unfortunately, and without exception, we will experience turbulent flights on occasion. The question is, do we have our seatbelts fastened with faith or unfastened in unbelief? If you are currently experiencing some unexpected turbulence in your life, be encouraged. We have a seat belt that will keep us safe until we have once again passed through the storm and into the clear blue skies. God has given us His rock, or seatbelt, which will allow us to weather the storm. All we have to do is wear it by faith, allowing the truth of His Word to give us strength and peace to ride out the turbulence and to ultimately stand in victory!

## PRAYER

Dear Lord, as I experience the turbulence of life, I thank You for Your Word that is eternal and true. Today I choose to walk by faith in Your Word, knowing You are faithful to accomplish all that You have begun in me. You will make all things work for my good because I love You and I'm called according to Your purpose. In Jesus's name. Amen.

## NOTES

_____

_____

_____

_____

_____

# NOTES

# DAY 14—THE APPROACH

Therefore, having been justified by faith, we have peace with God through
our Lord Jesus Christ, through whom also we have access by faith into
this grace in which we stand, and rejoice in hope of the glory of God. And
not only that, but we also glory in tribulations, knowing that tribulation
produces perseverance; and perseverance, character; and character,
hope. Now hope does not disappoint, because the love of God has been
poured out in our hearts by the Holy Spirit who was given to us.

—ROMANS 5:1-5

The weather at our destination is 100 feet overcast, and half-mile visibility, which is right at the ILS (instrument landing system) minimums. We are on top of the overcast at 30,000 feet, having a smooth ride in bright sunshine. At a little over 100 miles away, air traffic control tells us to cross a navigation fix that is 30 miles from the airport at 10,000 feet and at 250 knots indicated airspeed. I dial 10,000 feet into the flight control panel, push the knob, and the aircraft starts a programmed descent that will have it level at 10,000 feet and slowed to 250 knots at the proper time.

During the descent, my first officer gets the latest weather report and arrival gate information from another onboard computer. After four hours of nearly nothing happening, we are now getting busy for the arrival. I brief the arrival procedure along with the details of the ILS approach and verify that the information is properly loaded into the FMC (flight management computer). Passing 18,000 feet, I call for the Descent–Approach checklist. After completing that, the first officer makes a PA announcement to the passengers, thanking them for flying with us and giving them the latest weather at the airport.

We're in the clouds now and haven't seen anything since we entered them at 25,000 feet.

Approaching the 30-mile fix, the air traffic controller hands us off to the approach controller, who will vector us to the final approach course. After clearing us to 3,000 feet and slowing us to 180 knots indicated airspeed, he turns us to a 30-degree intercept angle to the final approach course. As we are slowing and turning, I call for flaps 1, followed shortly by flaps 2. The first officer responds by selecting the flaps 1 and 2 settings, which begins configuring the aircraft for landing. At about 3 miles from the glideslope (vertical flight indicator) intercept, the glideslope indicator starts coming down on the primary flight display, indicating that we are about to begin our final descent, and I call for the landing gear to be extended. Two miles from the glideslope intercept, I call out, "Flaps 3, Landing checklist," at which time she selects flaps 3, and we complete the landing checklist. At the glideslope intercept, I select the final approach speed of 140 knots. The autopilot has been tracking the localizer (horizontal course indicator) for about 5 miles and now captures the glideslope. I then call out, "Select missed approach altitude," just in case we have to execute a go-around. The first officer dials in the missed approach altitude of 4,000 feet into the flight control panel and calls the tower to get our landing clearance. Now our undivided attention is focused on monitoring our progress, speed, and altitude.

The radar altimeter barks out, "One thousand," and I confirm that the instruments are all lined up. I call out, "Stable," and we continue while still in the clouds.

Next, we hear the radar altimeter call out, "Five hundred." The first officer checks the instruments and responds, "Stable, target, sink 700," indicating that the aircraft is in a stable descent of 700 feet per minute and that we are at our target airspeed. So I continue the approach, still with no visual contact with the ground. At 300 feet, the first officer calls out, "One hundred above," and everything is still normal, so I respond, "Continuing." Then, just as the computer is about to announce, "Minimums," we break out of the overcast, the first officer sees the runway, and announces, "Runway in sight."

I look out and see the runway and call out, "Landing," and simultaneously disconnect the autopilot. As we get just above the runway, I ease the power back to idle thrust, and we land. After touchdown, I select reverse thrust and apply the brakes. As the aircraft slows to 80 knots, reverse thrust is deselected. We continue slowing to taxi speed and proceed to the gate for another on time arrival.

Reflecting on this approach, you can see how things got very busy and intense, and then, at the last minute, we broke out of the clouds and were able to land successfully. I'm reminded how this happens a lot as we fight life's battles. Perhaps you're in a spiritual battle and it seems like you're also in a dark cloud with no hope and no end in sight. I want to encourage you to continue your approach and stay on course; your breakthrough could be today. Years ago, I was going through a very difficult time with a relationship. I was always haunted by the fear of giving up the day before the breakthrough and missing a great spiritual victory. Well, I'm glad to say that the breakthrough came and that the relationship was completely restored literally overnight. Needless to say, I am very grateful I continued the approach and didn't give up. If I have one word of encouragement for you, it would be to *persevere*! The Bible says that the weapons of our warfare are mighty through God and that the enemy is defeated. Hold onto the Lord, stay in His Word, and surround yourself with other believers who will encourage you and help keep you on course.

Who knows? Tomorrow you might break out of the clouds and have the best landing ever!

## PRAYER

Heavenly Father, as I face the clouds of confusion and trials of life, I determine today to persevere by faith in You, knowing that You alone can keep me on course. Thank You for Your peace that You provide during those trials. Amen.

## NOTES

_____

_____

_____

_____

_____

_____

_____

_____

_____

_____

_____

_____

_____

_____

_____

# NOTES

_____

_____

_____

_____

_____

_____

_____

_____

_____

_____

_____

_____

_____

_____

_____

_____

_____

_____

_____

_____

_____

_____

_____

_____

# DAY 15—ZERO DARK THIRTY

I will praise You, For You have answered me,
And have become my salvation. The stone which the
builders rejected Has become the chief cornerstone. This
was the Lord's doing; It is marvelous in our eyes.
This is the day the Lord has made; We will rejoice and be glad in it.

— PSALM 118:21-24

It's early morning, just before sunrise on the last day of our three-day trip. As a crew, we'll go through the usual routine meeting downstairs to catch the hotel van to the airport. It's still dark, and I'm still in waking up mode. We arrive at the airport and make our way over to the TSA security checkpoint. After passing through security, we check in with the gate agent, and she gives us our release, which has our flight plan, weather reports, and other important flight information. She opens the door to the jetway, and we all make our way down to the aircraft. I'm fully awake now as I begin my checklists and prepare for the flight. We're fairly busy and not really aware of what's going on outside.

Right about then, the gate agent comes into the cockpit and, in a very excited voice, exclaims, "There's a beautiful sunrise this morning!" Having finished with my checklists, I grab my camera, step out of the jetway, and am met by a magnificent sunrise. The sky is blue, pink, and orange. It almost looks as if it is on fire and is reflected off the aircraft, giving it much the same appearance.

The scene was extremely powerful, and I was momentarily unable to move. It was as if the Lord painted this particular scene just to make me stop what I was doing and simply bask in His awesome Majesty! I did just that, and it completely changed my perspective for the rest of the day.

Are you in a hurry today, going through the same old routine and not really noticing the presence of the Lord? Perhaps He is saying to all of us that we need to step back, maybe even stop everything for just a few minutes, and realize that He is at work in every area of our lives. Let's slow down, observe, and soak in what He's providing just for us. Then we, like the psalmist, can say, "This is the day the Lord has made: we will rejoice and be glad in it." May His presence always be new and glorious all the days of our lives.

## PRAYER

Heavenly Father, thank You for revealing Yourself in so many wonderful ways. With the help of the Holy Spirit, I will look for You and be sensitive to Your presence in all areas my life, from this day forward. Show me Your glory today Lord. In Jesus's name. Amen.

## NOTES

_____

_____

_____

_____

_____

_____

_____

_____

_____

_____

# NOTES

_____

_____

_____

_____

_____

_____

_____

_____

_____

_____

_____

_____

_____

_____

_____

_____

_____

_____

_____

_____

_____

_____

_____

# DAY 16—REVISIONS

All Scripture is given by inspiration of God, and is profitable for doctrine,
for reproof, for correction, for instruction in righteousness, that the man
of God may be complete, thoroughly equipped for every good work.

—2 TIMOTHY 3:16–17

As pilots, we are always concerned with having up-to-date charts so that we can safely navigate. There are essentially two kinds of navigational charts that we use: the enroute chart and the approach chart. The enroute charts are much like the travel maps you might use in your car that take you from one city to the next. We also have approach charts, which are used to provide important information for landing on a particular runway. It should be pretty obvious that it could be quite dangerous to use an old approach chart that fails to provide updated information. Years ago, we would get revisions every week and have to sit down and meticulously go through all of our chart binders, locate the expired chart, open the binder, take out the old chart, and insert the new one. It was a painstaking but necessary process. Today those charts are all installed on an iPad, and the revising process is done in a matter of seconds by simply selecting the "update" prompt on the company app. It's a pilots dream come true because we all hated spending those many hours pulling pages out and putting pages in those binders.

Life, like those charts, is constantly in a state of revision, and while some revisions are good and welcome, many are not. Society and cultures are constantly revising standards in morals, actions, and behaviors that can be quite confusing to us as believers and damaging to humanity as a whole. Fortunately, our chart binder, the Bible, never changes; it has no revisions and no mistakes. In a time where the world is constantly changing what it considers acceptable, it's comforting to know we have a solid foundation from which to build our lives upon. Let's all encourage one another to stand firm in God's Word, knowing that it is inspired by God Himself and is to be used for our doctrine, correction, training in righteousness, and equipping us for our daily lives.

## PRAYER

Father, as the world around me seems to be changing in ways that that are sometimes confusing, I take refuge in Your unchanging Word. Thank you for Your chart binder that is sure, is never in need of revising, and always provides the course necessary to lead us to our ultimate destiny. Amen.

## NOTES

_____

_____

_____

_____

_____

_____

_____

_____

_____

_____

_____

_____

# NOTES

_____

_____

_____

_____

_____

_____

_____

_____

_____

_____

_____

_____

_____

_____

_____

_____

_____

_____

_____

_____

_____

_____

_____

# DAY 17—STANDARD OPERATING PROCEDURES

I say then: Walk in the Spirit, and you shall not fulfill the lust of the flesh.
For the flesh lusts against the Spirit, and the Spirit against the flesh; and
these are contrary to one another, so that you do not do the things that
you wish. But if you are led by the Spirit, you are not under the law.
Now the works of the flesh are evident, which are: adultery, fornication,
uncleanness, lewdness, idolatry, sorcery, hatred, contentions,
jealousies, outbursts of wrath, selfish ambitions, dissensions, heresies,
envy, murders, drunkenness, revelries, and the like; of which I tell
you beforehand, just as I also told you in time past, that those who
practice such things will not inherit the kingdom of God.
But the fruit of the Spirit is love, joy, peace, longsuffering, kindness,
goodness, faithfulness, gentleness, self-control. Against such there is no
law. And those who are Christ's have crucified the flesh with its passions
and desires. If we live in the Spirit, let us also walk in the Spirit. Let us
not become conceited, provoking one another, envying one another.

—GALATIANS 5:16-26

I just recently completed a three-day recurrent training course that
we are required to go through every nine months. No pilot I know
looks forward to those three days because they're quite intense and
mentally draining. The first day consists of several hours of classroom
instruction that mainly covers aircraft systems, company policies, and
discussing incidents and accidents that have occurred throughout the
entire airline industry, all with the goal of preventing them from
ever happening again. The next day is spent in a simulator, where we
review and practice normal and emergency procedures so we can
maintain our proficiency in maneuvers that we may be required to
perform in an actual emergency but are too dangerous and expensive
to practice in a real aircraft.

On the third day, we once again get in the simulator to simulate a flight from one city to the next while dealing with revised air traffic control clearances, mechanical malfunctions, changing weather conditions, and other issues, much as we experience in our normal flights. The purpose of that is to observe how the captain and first officer use all their available resources and also comply with SOPs (standard operating procedures). After those three days, there's a sense of relief that it's over and an incredible need to just decompress. The most important result is the renewed awareness that pilots are human and make mistakes. For years, pilots operated under the assumption that we just couldn't make mistakes. However, research has shown that mistakes are inevitable and that while we must attempt to avoid them, it is far more important that we have procedures in place to capture mistakes before they go too far and cause a problem. To help prevent any mistakes from continuing to the point of causing an accident, we have placed several barriers in our operation in an attempt to catch them. Some examples of those barriers are checklists, automation, and SOPs. Standard operating procedures are procedures that are used to standardize nearly all aspects of any flight. They allow thousands of pilots from all backgrounds and experience levels to know what to expect from one another even though they may have never previously flown together. Research has shown that almost all incidents occur because someone wasn't following SOPs.

God has given us some SOPs too. We are all familiar with God's moral laws found in the Ten Commandments. To the world, the Ten Commandments are relics from the past and are used to keep people from enjoying life. The truth is that the Ten Commandments are barriers that would, in most cases, prevent lives from crashing and being destroyed.

Paul goes into greater detail, giving us even more SOPs that are found in Galatians 5:16–25. He tells us to walk in the Spirit in order to avoid the lust of the flesh. He explains that the works as a flesh are adultery, fornication, hatred, murders, etc. Then he explains that the fruit of the Holy Spirit is, among other things, love, joy, and peace. They are proven and eternal. When we learn and practice these SOPs, we will be equipped by the Holy Spirit to handle every normal and emergency situation life will throw our way. I encourage us all to schedule some regular time with God and His Word so we can review and implement His SOPs. They are, after all, proven and eternal and will go a long way in providing a safe journey for us all.

## PRAYER

Heavenly Father, I thank You for Your Word that shows us how to live in ways that are both pleasing to You and life-changing for us. Help us to grow in the knowledge of Christ, submitting to Him and allowing Him to live in and through us. It's in His name that I pray. Amen.

## NOTES

_____

_____

_____

_____

_____

_____

_____

_____

_____

_____

_____

# NOTES

_____

_____

_____

_____

_____

_____

_____

_____

_____

_____

_____

_____

_____

_____

_____

_____

_____

_____

_____

_____

_____

_____

_____

_____

_____

_____

_____

# DAY 18—THE FLIGHT HOME

But now, thus says the Lord, who created you, O Jacob, And
He who formed you, O Israel: "Fear not, for I have redeemed
you; I have called you by your name; You are Mine.
When you pass through the waters, I will be with you; And through
the rivers, they shall not overflow you. When you walk through the
fire, you shall not be burned, Nor shall the flame scorch you.
For I am the Lord your God, The Holy One of Israel, your Savior.

—ISAIAH 43:1-3

It's been a long day, and I'm trying to catch the last flight home or else I will have to spend another night away from the bride. One of the greatest benefits of flying for an airline is the ability to live virtually anywhere and commute to work on a company flight for free. Of course, there is a catch: there must be an empty seat available. Still, for the most part, it works quite well.

Tonight the flight is booked full, and my only chance to get on it is if someone doesn't show. I've checked in with the gate agent, presented my credentials, and have been put on the standby list. Now it's a waiting game. Then, just before departure time arrives, I hear my name being called. I quickly grab my bags, run up to the agent, and get my boarding pass. I walk down the jetway to the pleasant smile of the flight attendant, who directs me to the only open seat on the aircraft. An hour and forty-five minutes later, we land at our destination. I made it. I'm home; another commute successfully completed. It's pretty routine, actually. I've been doing this for over thirty years. Of course, the commutes don't always end up like this, and sometimes I don't make the flight. The good news is that there's almost always an alternative way to get home, hopefully on the next flight.

There is another flight that I will have to make. In fact, we'll all have to make it. It's the final flight into eternity. The boarding process is quite similar. We have to board the correct flight by going through the correct jetway. That flight is eternal life, the jetway is the cross of Jesus Christ, and it all begins by hearing your name being called and responding to that call by faith. Maybe you're going through a time of uncertainty and fear in your life. If you have received Christ by faith, you already have a confirmed seat waiting for you. Hear the voice of God from Isaiah 43, "Fear not, for I have redeemed you; I have called you by name; you are mine." As good as it was to hear the gate agent call your name, that cannot compare to hearing God say, "Don't be afraid, I have redeemed you," (He redeemed you). "I have called you by name," (He called you). "You are mine," (He adopted you). And with that good news, I invite you to sit back, relax, and enjoy your flight!

## PRAYER

Dear Lord, the most beautiful words I could ever hear have been spoken to me by You: 'Don't be afraid, I have redeemed you. You are mine.' To think that the Creator of the universe has called me by name is beyond comprehension, and yet, I receive that truth by faith in the only one who could make it true, my Lord and Savior, Jesus Christ. Thank You, Father, for Your grace that promises that You will be with me during the floods and fires of life. Above all, Lord, thank You for the seat that is waiting for me on life's final flight, which will take me home to be with You forever. Amen.

## NOTES

_____

_____

_____

# NOTES

# DAY 19—EMERGENCY DESCENT

Let your conduct be without covetousness; be content with such things as
you have. For He Himself has said, "I will never leave you nor forsake you."

—HEBREWS 13:5

It's a beautiful day, and you're just past the halfway point of your
flight at 30,000 feet. The flight attendant has just served you another
cup of coffee, and you look out the window, reflecting on the success
of your business meeting and absorbing the beauty of the scenery
below. Suddenly, without any warning, the aircraft pitches down, and
the sound of the engines virtually disappears. Fear overwhelms you
as your mind races to try to make sense of it all. Next, your life passes
before you as memories from the past flash by in slow motion. The
dive seems to be lasting forever, and you have no doubt that this is the
end as you hear someone over the PA saying, "Emergency descent.
Remain seated."

On the flight deck, an entirely different scenario is taking place.
The pilots notice the cabin pressure is decreasing, causing the cabin
altitude to climb. If left unchecked, it will continue to climb to a point
where no one could survive the lack of oxygen. After following the
checklist, they are unable to correct the problem, so the captain calls
for an emergency descent. It is considered an emergency because the
pilots must get the air traffic controllers to clear all the altitudes below
them of any traffic and make sure that they have placed their oxygen
masks on. Although this is an emergency, it's one they have practiced
many times in flight simulators so they are in complete control of the
situation. They have their oxygen masks on and are communicating
with each other and with air traffic control, who has already begun

clearing traffic for their descent down to the safe altitude of 10,000 feet. The entire episode only lasts about four minutes and is complete before the passenger masks have a chance to automatically deploy in the cabin. After leveling off at 10,000 feet, the emergency is over. The pilots remove their masks, and the captain makes an announcement explaining what just happened and that the aircraft will be diverting to the nearest appropriate airport. The remainder of the flight is routine. In fact, the airport you have diverted to is a hub for the airline, and they already have another aircraft prepared for you to board and complete your flight to your original destination.

Have you ever experienced a time in your life when things seemed to be in a nosedive and completely out of control? You were possibly consumed with fear; then, after the situation passed, you realized that everything turned out fine because God was in control. We all go through times where nothing makes any sense whatsoever. Perhaps you're going through one now. Our Lord has given us some promises to hold onto during those scary times. First, He tells us that He will never forsake us (Hebrews 13:5), that He will be with us always (Matthew 28:20), and that when we experience tribulation, we can be encouraged because He has overcome the world (John 16:33). Finally, we can rest in the knowledge that all things work together for good to those who love God and are called according to His purpose (Romans 8:28). May we all have that peace when life's emergencies come our way, knowing that God is in total control and is always with us, especially during those times when we feel most alone! When that time comes, we can stand firm knowing that He is absolutely faithful and that His word is true.

## PRAYER

Heavenly Father, thank You for the promise of Your presence during all my trials and tribulations. Though I may not understand what is really occurring during those times, I know I can always rely on You to be with me, never, ever, forsaking me. For that, Lord, I will bless You and praise You all the days of my life. In Jesus's name. Amen.

## NOTES

# NOTES

# DAY 20—QUALIFIED

Therefore, if anyone is in Christ, he is a new creation; old things have passed away; behold, all things have become new. Now all things are of God, who has reconciled us to Himself through Jesus Christ, and has given us the ministry of reconciliation, that is, that God was in Christ reconciling the world to Himself, not imputing their trespasses to them, and has committed to us the word of reconciliation. Now then, we are ambassadors for Christ, as though God were pleading through us: we implore you on Christ's behalf, be reconciled to God. For He made Him who knew no sin to be sin for us, that we might become the righteousness of God in Him.

—2 CORINTHIANS 5:17-21

I am occasionally asked how I began my airline career and what my qualifications are. Well, the journey began in October 1973, in Pascagoula, Mississippi, at the Jackson County Airport. (You know you're getting to be an old pilot when the airport you learned to fly at no longer exists.) I was sixteen years old when I began taking lessons, and after reaching the age of seventeen, I earned my private pilot certificate. After that, I went on to earn the commercial pilot certificate, the instrument rating, the instructor rating, and instrument instructor rating. The instructor rating was crucial in that it allowed me to gain valuable experience and flight time while teaching others the joy of flying. Later, I was able to add the multi-engine and multi-engine instructor ratings. After graduation from the University of Mississippi, I landed a job in Montgomery, Alabama, as a flight instructor. After about a year, I began flying charter flights. It was during this time that I met the CEO of one of the larger banks in Alabama and was later hired to set up their corporate flight operation.

After about four and a half great years there, I was hired by USAir and began my airline career on May 5, 1986, with approximately 4,500 hours of flight time in my logbook. After several weeks of intense training, I passed the DC-9 first officer check ride. Since then, I have earned several type ratings, including the Boeing 737, 757, and 767, and the Airbus A-320 aircraft, and have also accumulated over 23,000 flight hours. Those are considered excellent qualifications, and yet, they are typical of most captains at any major airline. It also took several years and a great deal of effort to obtain those ratings.

While it's one thing to be qualified to fly large transport category aircraft, it's quite another to be qualified to be a child of God! There's also a big difference on how to become qualified. Are you struggling with the question of whether or not you're qualified to be a child of God? Maybe you feel as if you've done too much wrong to ever be qualified. Well, here's the bad news: none of us can ever get qualified, because God demands perfection. He demands perfect holiness. Don't despair, though, because according to Colossians 1:12, it is God Himself who qualifies us. John tells us that when we received Christ, that He gave us the right to become children of God (John 1:12). Finally, 1 Corinthians 5:21 says, "For He made Him who knew no sin to be sin for us, that we might become the righteousness of God in Him." Now read that verse again, slowly. To think that God made Christ, who knew no sin, to be sin, is in itself an inconceivable fact. But then He turns around and gives us His righteousness since we are in Christ! The fact is that you just can't get any more righteous than the righteousness of God! I don't know about you, but that gets me excited! If there ever was good news, this is it! That's the whole message of the cross: the fact that Jesus took all of our sin and gave us all of His righteousness. That's the great exchange! If you're feeling unworthy or like you have failed in your Christian walk, or even that you just don't measure up in your qualifications, be encouraged: God Himself has qualified you by His grace and your faith in Jesus Christ!

While it took me years and years of hard work and effort to become qualified to be an airline pilot, that pales in comparison to becoming a child of the living God, which can only be attained through God's grace as a free gift. So rise up, child of God, and walk, walk with a new spring in your step and joy in your heart. Because if God has qualified you, then you are absolutely qualified, and there is no one or nothing that could ever disqualify you!

## PRAYER

Heavenly Father, when I consider the truth of the cross and the exchanged life You offer through it, I can only fall on my face in gratitude and rise in new life that makes me more than a conqueror in all that life brings against me. Thank You for Your Word, that reminds me that while I was once a sinner saved by grace, I am now a child of the Living God! I am reminded yet again that I am an overcomer in Christ, and by faith in Him, I will continue to walk in victory for as long as I live. Amen.

## NOTES

_____

_____

_____

_____

_____

_____

_____

# NOTES

# DAY 21—RADAR CONTACT

O Lord, You have searched me and known me. You know my sitting
down and my rising up; You understand my thought afar off.
You comprehend my path and my lying down,
And are acquainted with all my ways.
For there is not a word on my tongue,
But behold, O Lord, You know it altogether.
You have hedged me behind and before,
And laid Your hand upon me.
Such knowledge is too wonderful for me;
It is high, I cannot attain it.
Where can I go from Your Spirit?
Or where can I flee from Your presence?
If I ascend into heaven, You are there;
If I make my bed in hell, behold, You are there.
If I take the wings of the morning,
And dwell in the uttermost parts of the sea,
Even there Your hand shall lead me,
And Your right hand shall hold me.
If I say, "Surely the darkness shall fall on me,"
Even the night shall be light about me;
Indeed, the darkness shall not hide from You,
But the night shines as the day;
The darkness and the light are both alike to You.
How precious also are Your thoughts to me, O God!
How great is the sum of them!
If I should count them, they would be more in number than the sand;
When I awake, I am still with You.
Search me, O God, and know my heart;
Try me, and know my anxieties;
And see if there is any wicked way in me,
And lead me in the way everlasting.

—PSALM 139:1-12, 17-18, 23-24

Today's flight is going from Charlotte, North Carolina, to Los Angeles, California. From the time we leave the gate through the time we pull up to the gate in Los Angeles, our aircraft will be in radar contact. Ground control has a radar that not only shows them that we're moving but also identifies the flight number so they will know exactly who we are. Once airborne, air traffic controllers will also know our ground speed and altitude. I can't say enough about how comforting it is to know someone has us in sight at all times and says to us, "Radar contact."

Psalm 139 brings us comfort in much the same way but on a much higher level. Going through life and feeling as if you're all alone is not a good feeling. Perhaps you feel that way right now, struggling with something or someone, seemingly all alone. Maybe you feel like God doesn't see you or, for that matter, doesn't even care. I know how you feel. I have been there myself. But take courage and be comforted because Psalm 139 tells us:

- That God has searched us and knows us!

- That He has His hedge of protection ahead and behind us and that His hand is upon us!

- That there is nowhere we can go that would separate us from His Spirit and His very presence!

- That even in utter darkness we are not hidden from Him!

- That His very thoughts are precious beyond comprehension, and infinite!

If you're going through a dark time in your life and you feel like God doesn't even know where you are or what you're going through, I encourage you to read this psalm and focus on just how much the Lord does, in fact, know about you and where you are. You could even pray the last two verses, "Search me, O God, and know my heart; try me and know my anxieties; and see if any wicked way is in me, and lead me in the way everlasting." Then you too will know that He knows everything about you. Rest assured because the truth is that you are in radar contact!

## PRAYER

Heavenly Father, as I go through times of trouble and uncertainty, I am so thankful that I am on your radar screen and always in Your presence. Thank You for giving me that peace that only You can give, that peace that passes all understanding. Amen.

## NOTES

# NOTES

# DAY 22—THROUGH THE STORMS

Then He said to His disciples, "Therefore I say to you, do not worry about your life, what you will eat; nor about the body, what you will put on. Life is more than food, and the body is more than clothing. Consider the ravens, for they neither sow nor reap, which have neither storehouse nor barn; and God feeds them. Of how much more value are you than the birds? And which of you by worrying can add one cubit to his stature? If you then are not able to do the least, why are you anxious for the rest? Consider the lilies, how they grow: they neither toil nor spin; and yet I say to you, even Solomon in all his glory was not arrayed like one of these. If then God so clothes the grass, which today is in the field and tomorrow is thrown into the oven, how much more will He clothe you, O you of little faith? "And do not seek what you should eat or what you should drink, nor have an anxious mind. For all these things the nations of the world seek after, and your Father knows that you need these things. But seek the kingdom of God, and all these things shall be added to you."

—LUKE 12:22-31

Tonight, I'm sitting at the dinner table in Tampa, reflecting on today's flight. We had earlier flown from Charlotte to Cancun and then back to Charlotte. We then went through customs and back through security and on to our next plane. There was still plenty of time to check the weather for our flight to Tampa. Frankly, after looking at the forecast and the weather radar, it appeared getting to Tampa was going to be a bit of a challenge. There would be no problem for the first half of the flight, but the second half, and especially Tampa itself, looked ripe for some developing lines of severe thunderstorms.

We took off and climbed up to 30,000 feet. Then, just as advertised, thunderstorms appeared on our planned route of flight. A few minutes later, air traffic control gave us a reroute, which took us well west of our normal route in order to avoid the developing thunderstorms. They informed us that we might be holding as we approached the Tampa airport. Anytime we are told to anticipate holding, our attention goes straight to our fuel situation. No matter what happens, we must plan to have enough fuel to go to our destination, attempt to land, climb back to a specified altitude, proceed to our alternate airport, and arrive there and still have our reserve fuel on board. That fuel requirement compared to the fuel on the aircraft will determine how long we can hold. Fortunately, after slowing down to a significantly reduced speed, we were able to buy enough time and didn't have to hold. That was welcome news. However, the weather ahead of us looked as though it might still be a little turbulent, so I made an announcement reminding the passengers to remain seated with their seatbelts fastened. I also reassured them that if we saw that it was unsafe to continue to Tampa, we would not hesitate to divert to our alternate. Next, I called the flight attendants and told them to prepare the cabin for landing as quickly as possible and to return to their seats so they wouldn't get hurt if we encountered any turbulence. Shortly after that, we broke out of the weather at about 13,000 feet. The rest of the flight was perfectly smooth.

Life is very similar in that we look around and see problems everywhere. Maybe it's concerns with the economy, our job, or relationships with family and friends. Perhaps it is the international unrest and terrorism that keeps us awake at night. Sometimes things appear to be totally hopeless and then, after a bit of time passes, we realize that things were resolved smoothly and uneventfully. In fact, with just a bit of thought, we could see where God worked it all out and that our worrying was for nothing. Believe me, I know that feeling, and I know you would agree with me when I tell you it's not a fun place to be. The good news is we have a God who is well aware of our needs, who is here with us and is more than able to meet those needs.

In Luke 12, Jesus reminds us that worry will not add a single hour to our lives. He then reminds us that God feeds the birds, and yet, we are infinitely more valuable to Him than birds. He then asks this incredible question: "If God clothes the grass of the field, which is here today, and tomorrow is thrown into the fire, how much more will He clothe you?" Finally, He reminds us to seek first the kingdom of God and all our needs will be taken care of. Could it be that the reasons our mountains turn out to be molehills is because God makes it so? I don't know what your situation is, but I do know that every time I've ever focused on God and His kingdom, He calms the storms in my life, and I can look back and see His hand in all.

## PRAYER

Dear Lord, as I encounter the storms of life, help me remember that worry will add nothing to my life and that the important thing is to seek Your kingdom first and all my needs will be met. Lord, You alone offer hope in a hopeless situation, and for that, I give You praise. In Jesus's name. Amen.

## NOTES

_____

_____

_____

_____

_____

_____

_____

# NOTES

_____

_____

_____

_____

_____

_____

_____

_____

_____

_____

_____

_____

_____

_____

_____

_____

_____

_____

_____

_____

_____

_____

# DAY 23—BEHIND THE SCENES

Suddenly, a hand touched me, which made me tremble on my knees and on
the palms of my hands. And he said to me, "O Daniel, man greatly beloved,
understand the words that I speak to you, and stand upright, for I have now
been sent to you." While he was speaking this word to me, I stood trembling.
Then he said to me, "Do not fear, Daniel, for from the first day that you set
your heart to understand, and to humble yourself before your God, your words
were heard; and I have come because of your words. But the prince of the
kingdom of Persia withstood me twenty-one days; and behold, Michael, one
of the chief princes, came to help me, for I had been left alone there with the
kings of Persia. Now I have come to make you understand what will happen to
your people in the latter days, for the vision refers to many days yet to come."
When he had spoken such words to me, I turned my face
toward the ground and became speechless.

—DANIEL 10:10-15

The airline I work for operates nearly 6,700 flights per day to
destinations all over the world. You can imagine that the amount
of behind-the-scenes activities are mind-boggling and that it takes
a virtual army of around 100,000 people to make it happen. It goes
without saying that every job is important to the successful outcome
of your flight. From the time you book your reservation until the time
you retrieve your bags at your destination, a highly choreographed
operation takes place involving everyone from the aircraft cleaners
who keep your aircraft clean to the mechanics who go through the
aircraft performing countless checks to ensure it will operate in
complete safety. There are baggage handlers who load and unload
your bags, many times having them on the carousel in baggage claim
before you arrive to retrieve them. There are dispatchers who plan
your flight, taking into consideration the weather, fuel load, and
flight conditions for passenger comfort and fuel efficiencies. They

will also provide the flight crew with a flight release, which contains the filed flight plan information and any special advisories for that flight. This activity doesn't even begin to scratch the surface of all it takes to make your flight successful. To think it happens 6,700 times a day is truly amazing!

Now there is a much larger and more powerful behind-the-scenes army involved and making your life victorious! In several places, the Bible describes a battle that goes on in the spirit realm that is manifested in the natural realm. In the book of Daniel, we see where Daniel had been praying to God without obtaining an answer when an angel suddenly appeared to him and explained why the answer had been delayed. He explained that God heard his prayers from the first day but that the prince of Persia (more than likely a territorial demonic host), withstood him for twenty-one days. Finally, Michael, the archangel (the chief prince of angels), came to help the angel overcome the prince of Persia (Daniel 10).

When we come upon people and situations that are difficult, we can be encouraged, knowing that our prayers are answered. And when it seems they aren't, we can walk in faith, knowing that our struggle is not against flesh and blood, but against the rulers, authorities, and powers of darkness in the spirit realm. The good news is that the angelic hosts far outnumber the demonic ones. Better yet, we have the risen Christ living in us through the indwelling of the Holy Spirit. In fact, Paul reminds us that we are more than conquerors through Christ (Romans 8:37)!

So, just as the airline has a massive supporting force working behind the scenes for your flight, our God has an infinitely larger and more powerful supporting force behind us. Be encouraged, no matter what you may be going through. Remember this: we are not fighting for victory; instead, we are, in fact, fighting from victory!

## PRAYER

Heavenly Father, thank You for reminding me that I am not alone and that there are legions of angels warring on my behalf and that, above all, Jesus Christ is living in and through me, making me a victor in life. Amen.

## NOTES

# NOTES

# DAY 24—THE FLIGHT PLAN

*You stiff-necked and uncircumcised in heart and ears! You
always resist the Holy Spirit; as your fathers did, so do you.*

—ACTS 7:51

Things have changed a lot over the years in how we navigate
airplanes. When I came to the airline in 1986, I flew the DC-9,
which was based on the 1960's technology. Our system of navigation
was ground-based, using very high-frequency, omni-directional
radios, known as VORs. Essentially, they are simply radio stations
placed all around the country that made 360 radials extending
outward from the station much like spokes of a wheel, each making
up 1-degree courses that work reasonably well. As pilots, we would
select a heading to fly the beam, or radial, to or from the VOR,
keeping the aircraft on that beam by changing the heading to correct
for the wind. The problem was that as you traveled further from the
station, the width of the beam grew, making it possible to be a few
miles off course. Still, it was more than accurate enough for en route
navigation. Today, we use the GPS, which keeps us within just a few
feet of our planned course. In fact, on a typical flight, I will select
the navigation function of the autopilot shortly after takeoff, and the
airplane will follow the entire route all the way to the destination.

If at any time during the flight, I need to alter the course, I simply
reach up, twist the heading selector knob to a desired heading, and
the 205,000-pound aircraft will immediately respond and turn to
whatever heading I select. Then to get back on course, I type the
navigational fix into the navigation computer, and the autopilot will
immediately turn us on a course that will take us to that fix. The

thought occurred to me that God has a flight plan for us. He even has a navigation chart for us to use called the Bible. Life's worst problems occur when we disregard our navigation chart and venture off course. When our heavenly Father selects the heading to put us back on course, how often do we respond? I must confess that there have been many times in my life that I did not respond, which has caused me to experience periods of turbulence in my life. What about you? Can you look back in your past and find some storms that could have been avoided if only you had responded to God's course corrections? In reality, that's a universal problem for all of us.

In Acts 7, Stephen gives the Jewish leaders a brief history lesson and then concludes it by telling them that they were "stiff-necked" (stubborn) and that they resisted the Holy Spirit. What was their reaction? They were offended and stoned him to death. What about us? What will our response be when God corrects us? Will we be offended? Will we resist the Holy Spirit? My prayer for all of us is that we will constantly use the Bible to check our course, ask God for direction, and be sensitive to the leading of the Holy Spirit in obedience to God's course correction. This is the only way we can stay on course. Being human, we will make a wrong turn here and there, but as long as we listen and obey when we hear, we will get back on course. Is God changing our course today? If He is, let's not resist but respond immediately and stay on course so we will arrive at the destiny He has chosen for us!

### PRAYER

Thank You, Lord, that You reveal the course You desire for me, and that when I do deviate, You are faithful to show the way back on course. Help me be sensitive to Your leading through the Holy Spirit so I can stay on course. In Jesus's name. Amen.

# NOTES

_____

_____

_____

_____

_____

_____

_____

_____

_____

_____

_____

_____

_____

_____

_____

_____

_____

_____

_____

_____

_____

_____

# DAY 25—ATTITUDE AND ALTITUDE

Have you not known?
Have you not heard?
The everlasting God, the Lord,
The Creator of the ends of the earth,
Neither faints nor is weary.
His understanding is unsearchable.
He gives power to the weak,
And to those who have no might, He increases strength.
Even the youths shall faint and be weary,
And the young men shall utterly fall,
But those who wait on the Lord
Shall renew their strength;
They shall mount up with wings like eagles,
They shall run and not be weary,
They shall walk and not faint.

—ISAIAH 40:28-31

The most exciting and critical time of any flight is the takeoff. Many people think that the takeoff is nothing more than pushing the throttles forward, going fast, and it's off into the wild blue yonder. In fact, there's a great deal of planning and specific procedures in place to help ensure that every takeoff is safe, even in the event of an engine failure.

To begin with, we have to consider the weight of the aircraft, air temperature, surface winds, and runway length, among other things, prior to every takeoff. Once all those variables are considered, we can compute three critical speeds for takeoff. These speeds are referred to as:

1) V1: Decision Speed. If anything critical happens prior to this speed, the takeoff is aborted and the airplane stops on the remaining length of runway. Beyond this speed, if something goes wrong, the takeoff is continued.

2) Vr: Rotation Speed. This is the speed at which we raise the nose of the aircraft (rotate) and actually begin to fly.

3) V2: Takeoff Safety Speed. This is the speed flown in the event of an engine failure after V1 that will allow a safe climb.

The typical takeoff begins at the departure gate, when we complete the final performance calculations. Once cleared for takeoff, the pilot flying will set the power to the computed thrust setting, and the monitoring pilot will confirm the thrust setting is properly set. When we accelerate through 80 knots, the monitoring pilot will say, "Eighty."

The flying pilot will confirm his airspeed indicator also indicates 80 knots and respond, "Check." This confirms that both pilots' airspeed indicators are functioning properly and tells us that we have entered into the critical phase of the takeoff and will only reject the takeoff in the event of a critical failure.

We continue accelerating to V1 (approximately 140 knots), and the monitoring pilot calls out, "V1," which means we are committed to go in the event of an emergency because there is insufficient runway to stop the aircraft. Next comes the rotation speed, or Vr. At Vr, the monitoring pilot says, "Rotate." The pilot flying pulls back slightly on the control stick and points the nose up, which causes the airplane to climb.

When the pilot monitoring notices a positive rate of climb, he will say, "Positive rate," and the pilot flying will say, "Gear up." The monitoring pilot raises the gear by saying, "Gear up," select the "up" position on the landing gear control lever, and confirming that the wheels came up properly.

Then, at 1,000 feet above the ground, the pilot flying will accelerate to 250 knots, which is the maximum allowable indicated airspeed below 10,000 feet above sea level. During this period of acceleration, the flap retraction speed is reached, and the flying pilot will say, "Flaps up. After takeoff checklist." The monitoring pilot will complete the after takeoff checklist and announce, "After takeoff checklist complete." Once that's done, we can sit back and relax a bit as we enter the en route climb phase of the flight.

In all of this, the one thing that is most critical in making the aircraft fly is to put it into the correct flight attitude, which is to raise the nose to the correct climb attitude. Simply put, the plane's attitude helps determine its altitude. The same is true for us. If we want to climb above our circumstances we must lift our attitudes. If you're down and out and depressed, you will not rise above your circumstances. Thankfully, we are not without hope. Psalm 43:5 addresses that very issue: "Why, my soul, are you downcast? Why so disturbed within me? Put your hope in God, I will yet praise Him, my Savior and my God." Habakkuk 3:17–18 adds, "Though the fig tree does not bud and there are no grapes on the vine, though the olive crop fails and the fields produce no food, though there are no sheep in the pen and no cattle in the stalls, yet I will rejoice in the Lord, I will be joyful in God my savior."

We are not without hope; we worship a God who will never leave us or forsake us. Be encouraged. Through Christ, we truly have the ability to lift up our eyes and rise above our circumstances, no matter what they may be.

## PRAYER

Father God, some days it seems impossible to even get off the ground, much less fly. Help me lift up my countenance and fly far above any circumstance that is weighing me down. I thank You, Lord, for Your Word, which encourages me and reminds me that I can do all things through Christ. Amen.

## NOTES

# NOTES

# DAY 26—CONTRAILS

Behold, I will do a new thing,
Now it shall spring forth;
Shall you not know it?
I will even make a road in the wilderness
And rivers in the desert.

—ISAIAH 43:19

Have you ever stood outside and looked up to see several white trails crossing each other in the sky? These are contrails left by aircraft at high altitude. Sometimes they aren't very long and dissipate in a few short minutes, and at other times, they stretch for miles and last for quite some time. Contrails are condensation trails that are formed when extremely hot exhaust gases from the engine come in contact with the very cold air found at high altitudes. For the most part, the temperature and moisture content determines how long contrails last. You can always tell where the aircraft was by referencing the contrail.

There is an interesting fact about contrails and aircraft. They will always show where the aircraft has been and the direction it's headed; however, not exactly where it's going or its final destination. You could say that contrails reflect the recent past of the aircraft.

Just as the plane has a past, we all have a past too. Maybe your past has been less than stellar or even horrendous. Maybe you have made more than your share of mistakes and believe your past or your contrail is determining your destiny. Well, I have some good news for you!

While your past mistakes may have greatly influenced your journey so far, they need not determine your destiny!

The Bible has many examples of men who made mistakes but, by the grace of God, ended up with a great destiny. David was guilty of committing adultery and murder, yet God redeemed him and even made him a king. Zacchaeus was a despised tax collector who, upon encountering Jesus, became a follower and restored fourfold those from whom he had stolen. Then there was Saul, who persecuted Christians even to the point of allowing them to be murdered. After coming into contact with the risen Christ, he became known as Paul the apostle to the gentiles, spreading the gospel of grace and writing two-thirds of the New Testament.

So while your past indicates where we have been, it has no power to determine our destinies. In fact, just as contrails dissipate and go away, in God's eyes, our past is also erased, never to be remembered again! 2 Corinthians 5:17 tells us that if we're in Christ, then we're a new creation, that the old is past, and the new is here. In Isaiah 43:25 and Hebrews 10:17, God says He will remember our sin no more! Be encouraged; we've all sinned and made mistakes. Some may have even been quite serious. However, with Christ, we don't focus on our contrails. Instead, we allow Him to take control and turn our attention to our new destiny, the destiny of abundant and eternal life!

## PRAYER

Heavenly Father, when I recall my past, I am amazed at Your Word, which reminds me of the phenomenal mercy and grace You extend to me every day. Thank You, Lord, that the destiny You've given me is infinitely greater than the past I have given You. Amen.

# NOTES

_____

_____

_____

_____

_____

_____

_____

_____

_____

_____

_____

_____

_____

_____

_____

_____

_____

_____

_____

_____

_____

_____

_____

_____

# DAY 27—REROUTE

But as it is written: "Eye has not seen, nor ear heard, Nor have entered into the heart of man The things which God has prepared for those who love Him."
— 1 CORINTHIANS 2:9

Prior to departing Los Angeles for the redeye to Charlotte, I looked at the weather on my computer and saw a line of severe thunderstorms that stretched from southern Louisiana all the way up to Indiana. Normally, our route would take us over Nashville on the way to Charlotte from Los Angeles. Unfortunately, that route would take us through the middle of the severe weather, something I certainly wasn't going to do.

I called the dispatcher and requested and received a reroute that went to New Orleans, then to Pensacola, and finally northeast toward Atlanta and Charlotte. Although this would add about twenty minutes to the flight, it was certainly much better than trying to go through what appeared to be a very serious line of thunderstorms. At about 4:30 in the morning, we flew over New Orleans and watched one of the most vivid displays of lightning I've ever seen just north of our position. The reroute paid off as we remained in the clear with a smooth ride and arrived in Charlotte only fifteen to twenty minutes late. It was a small price to pay in order to avoid what certainly would have been a very turbulent flight.

Sometimes God gives us a reroute, though in reality, for Him, it's not a reroute at all. Have you ever experienced a delay in a personal goal or answered prayer? Sometimes He will change our course to protect us, much like when I changed our course to avoid the dangerous weather on that flight. In Matthew 2, God told Joseph and Mary to flee to Egypt to avoid Herod, who ultimately had ordered every male child under the age of two murdered in an attempt to protect his throne from the perceived threat from this newborn baby who was born the king of the Jews. In essence, the family was rerouted to Nazareth by way of Egypt to avoid the murderous hand of King Herod. In this case, they were protected from danger by being separated from Herod.

At other times, God gives us a reroute to prepare us for what's ahead. For example, in Galatians 1, we see where Paul didn't go to Jerusalem to confer with the other apostles for a period of three years. Instead, he went to Arabia, to be prepared by the risen Christ for his ministry to the gentiles.

Are you experiencing a reroute and don't understand why? Maybe it's for separation from harm from the adversary or maybe it's for preparation for something beyond your normal ability. The fact is that you may not know for some time. You can know this, though: If God is protecting you, you will never be safer. And if He's preparing you, you will never be better prepared! Rejoice in your reroute because our heavenly Father always has something prepared for us that is beyond our imagination!

## PRAYER

Dear Lord, I determine today to walk in faith, believing Your hand is directly involved in my life, and that every reroute You provide has a purpose that will ultimately work for my good and is, in fact, beyond my imagination. Thank you, Lord. In Jesus's name. Amen.

## NOTES

---

---

# NOTES

# DAY 28—CHANGE

I beseech you therefore, brethren, by the mercies of God, that you
present your bodies a living sacrifice, holy, acceptable to God, which
is your reasonable service. And do not be conformed to this world,
but be transformed by the renewing of your mind, that you may
prove what is that good and acceptable and perfect will of God.

—ROMANS 12:1-2

As pilots, we have procedures for nearly everything we do. It is a way of maintaining safety; but, just as important, having procedures spelled out for us gives us a high level of consistency in our day-to-day operations. With over 15,000 pilots, you can imagine the confusion on the flight deck if no one knew exactly what to expect from one another. Also, once you get familiar with company procedures, things tend to get comfortable and routine, which causes interactions with another pilot to be almost second nature, even though you've never met each other prior to the trip.

Recently, after our merger with another airline, we had to learn new operating procedures, which in many ways, were very different from ours. The goal in any merger, operationally speaking, is to get two different companies to become one company with a seamless network where everyone is on the same page. That entails change, sometimes lots of change. Pilots, especially older pilots like myself, resist change. The reality, however, is that if we don't change, we don't fly—so, well, we change. Once we get familiar with the new procedures they too become second nature.

Once we merge into the family of God as His adopted children, we soon realize quite another change occurs from within. We become aware that we belong to a whole new kingdom with a whole new way of living. As we study God's Word and get to know Him, we start to see a new set of values, values that are, in many ways, radically different from the ones we had prior to receiving Christ. For example, Jesus tells us in Matthew 5:43–48 that we are to love our enemies. Another example is found in Matthew 6:19–21, where He tells us to lay up treasures in heaven rather than on earth because heavenly treasures can't be stolen or destroyed since they are eternal. There are many more changes that come through this merger, some that are easy, and, frankly, some that are difficult. The good news is that as we renew our minds (Romans 12:1–2), we will be transformed, our thinking will change, and, therefore, our actions will change. It's a lifelong process of learning God's procedures, but as we do, they will also become second nature. Let us always reflect on our thoughts and actions as compared to the Word of God. How do your thoughts today compare with thoughts from years ago? Perhaps more important, how will your thoughts change tomorrow and beyond? The more we renew our minds in accordance with scripture, the more our thoughts and actions will line up with God's desires. Ultimately, as we grow in grace, God's desires will also be our desires, making us more like Him. And it all begins with one simple thing: change.

## PRAYER

Heavenly Father, as I look back on my life, I am amazed at the changes in my thinking that have occurred over the years. While some of the changes were easy, some were more difficult, and others seem nearly impossible. And yet I realize they were all for my benefit. Thank You, Lord, for Your patience as I continue to merge the life I have lived with the one You have planned. Amen.

NOTES

_____

_____

_____

_____

_____

_____

_____

_____

_____

_____

_____

_____

_____

_____

_____

_____

_____

_____

_____

_____

_____

_____

_____

_____

# DAY 29—ENDURANCE

Therefore, brethren, having boldness to enter the Holiest by the blood of Jesus,
by a new and living way which He consecrated for us, through the veil, that
is, His flesh, and having a High Priest over the house of God, let us draw near
with a true heart in full assurance of faith, having our hearts sprinkled from
an evil conscience and our bodies washed with pure water. Let us hold fast
the confession of our hope without wavering, for He who promised is faithful.
And let us consider one another in order to stir up love and good works, not
forsaking the assembling of ourselves together, as is the manner of some, but
exhorting one another, and so much the more as you see the Day approaching.

—HEBREWS 10:19-25

As pilots, one of the biggest considerations we must plan for is
how much fuel we'll need for the trip. Unlike with the family
car, we rarely fill the fuel tanks completely because of the added
weight. For every flight, we need to consider taxi fuel and the fuel for
takeoff, climb, cruise, descent, and landing. In addition to that, we
need enough fuel for route changes that may arise due to weather.
Then we add fuel for holding in case traffic or weather becomes a
factor at our destination. Finally, if the destination weather is forecast
to be an issue, we add enough fuel to divert to an alternate airport.
Then, after all of that, we add our reserve fuel. It's not uncommon to
fly a one-hour leg and yet have enough fuel to be able to fly for four
hours. So you can see we are not as concerned with the miles we can
fly as we are with how long we can fly, or in other words, how much
endurance we have.

Life also requires endurance. If jet fuel determines our plane's
endurance, what determines our personal endurance as believers?
When life brings storms, turbulence, delays, and disappointments,

how do we endure? The writer in Hebrews speaks of our need for endurance. In chapter 10, he explains how Christ has so completely satisfied God's will that He set aside the old covenant and establish the new, causing us to be sanctified once and for all through the offering of the body of Christ. Hebrews 10:22–25 gives us steps to ensure that we obtain the endurance we need for life:

1) Draw near to God with a sincere heart and the full assurance that faith brings, having our hearts sprinkled to cleanse us from a guilty conscience. Daily, we need to draw close to our heavenly Father through prayer and spending time in His Word, listening for His voice.

2) Hold unswervingly to the hope we profess, knowing He who promised is faithful. We can rest assured that God is faithful and will accomplish all that He promises in His Word. We can hold on to that hope in spite of any circumstances that we may be going through. His faithfulness is our rock-solid foundation that will not be shaken, no matter what storms may come our way.

3) Push each other toward love and good deeds. Another source of fuel for the journey is the love that we have for one another. In fact, Jesus said that the world would know us by the love we have for one another. That love, in many cases, is manifested through good deeds. Those deeds may consist of physical deeds or even just being there for others and offering encouragement when needed.

4) Continue meeting together. Some people believe that you have to go to church to please God and that if they miss church, God will be angry with them. That's just not the case. Now having said that, I am in no way minimizing the need to be in church and to be involved with a church. However, the purpose of being involved in a church is

so that we can be edified and also help edify others. Just as an ember that is removed from a fire will cool off, so will a believer run low on fuel if he or she doesn't fellowship with other believers.

5) Encourage one another. Finally, we all need encouragement. We are all going through things that can wear us down and even defeat us. As believers, we should not operate alone but, in fact, we should be a vital part of the body of Christ along with other believers in order to strengthen one another. While it is true that we can do all things through Christ who strengthens us, we are still human. We all have bad days and need others to pick us up and keep us on course so that we can reach the goal that is set before us. We have all had days where just a word of encouragement radically changed our attitude. You may need a word of encouragement today; better yet, maybe you could be the one who gives the word of encouragement to someone else, making that person's day far brighter than it would have been otherwise.

If we do these things, we will all endure, no matter what life throws at us!

## PRAYER

Heavenly Father, thank You for sending others into my life to help build me up so that I can endure, and not merely endure, but be victorious! Help me be sensitive to the needs of others so that I may be an encourager to them. In Jesus's name. Amen.

## NOTES

_____

_____

_____

# NOTES

_____

_____

_____

_____

_____

_____

_____

_____

_____

_____

_____

_____

_____

_____

_____

_____

_____

_____

_____

_____

_____

_____

_____

_____

_____

# DAY 30—THRUST

John answered, saying to all, "I indeed baptize you with water; but
One mightier than I is coming, whose sandal strap I am not worthy
to loose. He will baptize you with the Holy Spirit and fire.

—LUKE 3:16

How many times have you looked at the engine just outside the window of your aircraft and wondered how in the world it works. It just seems like air goes in the front and exits out the back, resulting in an increase in two things: noise and speed. What happens inside is a complete mystery. Actually, it's a fairly simple system. The jet engine is made up of many different stages of fan blades, which, as they spin, compress the air into the engine. Once that air is combined with fuel, a flame is introduced, causing the air to heat up to extremely high temperatures. This intense heat causes the rapidly expanding air to exhaust out the back end of the engine, which creates thrust. When you introduce more fuel by increasing the throttle setting, you introduce more heat. An increase in heat causes the compressor blades to increase air volume, which causes an increase in thrust. Because a jet engine only spins, it is a much smoother operation than piston engines of days gone by. Even though they operate in extreme heat from the burning of the fuel, they are far more reliable and powerful than those old piston engines.

Without the heat caused from the flame that is introduced to the compressed air, there would be no thrust and therefore no flight. In many ways, life is similar to the operation of the jet. Throughout our lives, we will, from time to time, experience pressure from events that occur. At times, that pressure will become very intense, even painful.

Rest assured that God's purpose in our lives is to move us forward and climb to the heights He has destined us for. He has also provided a hot fire that will handle the pressure and thrust us forward toward that destiny. The fire I'm writing about is the fire of the Holy Spirit, the Comforter, the Teacher, the one who gives us power to overcome the world. John the Baptist told the people that he came to baptize with water but that Jesus would baptize us with fire, the fire of the Holy Spirit. That very fire is available for us today and is received by faith.

Another law of aerodynamics tells us that drag increases exponentially as airspeed increases. For many years the speed of sound was considered an impenetrable barrier. In fact, it was called the *sound barrier*. As I mentioned, many scientists and aviators considered the sound barrier impossible to exceed. Then, on October 14, 1947, a pilot named Chuck Yeager broke the sound barrier in his rocket-powered plane, the X-1, the *Glamorous Glennis*, named after his wife, Glennis. An interesting fact is that the drag he experienced was at its greatest peak just before breaking the sound barrier. Many times, the same is true in our spiritual battles. I know that in my own life, one of my greatest breakthroughs occurred during what seemed to be the lowest point in my spiritual battle.

Perhaps today you're feeling intense pressure because the world and the enemy of your soul is applying forces that seem to be overwhelming you. You may even feel like you are at the end of your rope, and you just want to give up and let go. Please consider that it very well could be that this is just what God wants you to experience so that He can show you and those who know you that it's His power, and His power alone, that breaks the spiritual barrier and brings victory. Be encouraged; Jesus said that He has overcome the world, and Scripture reminds us that greater is He who is in us than he who is in the world.

The fact is that without resistance or trials, we would never be tested, and without testing, we would never grow in strength and power. We would never know or experience the promises of God that tell us we are more than conquerors through Christ.

So just as the jet engine experiences great pressure and needs the heat of fire within that engine to produce thrust, we, as children of God, can also allow the fire of the Holy Spirit to deal with life's situations and pressures. We can experience the thrust needed to overcome the resistance of the enemy and fly far above our circumstances, farther in fact, than we ever could alone!

## PRAYER

Heavenly Father, thank You for the fire of the Holy Spirit that empowers me to rise above all my circumstances. Help me to see my situations from Your perspective and know that although You may not be the author of my battle, You are certainly the author of my victory! For that, Lord, I give You all the glory and honor. In Jesus's mighty name. Amen!

## NOTES

# NOTES

_____

_____

_____

_____

_____

_____

_____

_____

_____

_____

_____

_____

_____

_____

_____

_____

_____

_____

_____

_____

_____

_____

_____

_____

# ABOUT THE AUTHOR

CAPTAIN GREG JOHNSTON flies the Airbus A-321 for American Airlines. He resides in Pascagoula, Mississippi with his wife, Beth. Greg began flying in October, 1973 at the age of 16. He began instructing student pilots while in College at the University of Mississippi. After obtaining his degree, he moved to Montgomery, Alabama where he began his career working up the ranks as a flight instructor, charter pilot, and corporate pilot. Finally, in May of 1986, he was hired by USAir and began flying as a first officer on the DC-9. In 1988 Greg flew a trip with a captain who shared his faith and stirred his interest. It was after that trip that he began seeking God, and while reading John's gospel, received Christ as his personal Savior.